Winchester

Seventy-eight Local Businesses, Artists and Producers

THE WINCHESTER GUIDEBOOK

By Kyle Alexander

Copyright © K. S. Alexander 2020
All content, text and imagery © K. S. Alexander 2020

First published in Great Britain in 2020 by K. S. Alexander

ISBN 978-1-5272-5552-4

Photography by Kyle Alexander, Ozzi Sanderson & Oscar Ferguson
Typesetting & Design: Curtis Rayment
Cover Page: G. F. Smith Colorplan, Citrine, 270gsm
Type: Forma DJR Text & Adobe Garamond

Printed in Great Britain

By R.F.A

www.thewinchesterguidebook.com

ISBN 978-1-5272-5552-4

9 781527 255524 >

PREFACE

To the modern traveller, Winchester is defined by its history. It was the home of English kings and the power base of bishops; a centre for great rulers, as well as great romantic minds. But I assume that you have done your historical homework, and so instead, I offer you an alternative cultural perspective. Here, in these pages, lies an insight into the present-day city, and the likings of its current crop. From the favoured shops and social spots, to the chophouses, hotels and hostelries. Where we eat, where we drink, and where we buy our tea bags. Welcome to Winchester.

CONTENTS

LOCAL PRODUCERS

OFFICIAL PARTNERS

INTRODUCTION

"We like it very much: it is the pleasantest Town I ever was in, and has the most recommendations of any. There is a fine Cathedral...part of it built 1400 years ago; and the more modern by a magnificent Man called William of Wickham...The whole town is beautifully wooded. From the Hill at the eastern extremity you see a prospect of Streets, and old Buildings mixed up with Trees. Then there are the most beautiful streams about I ever saw – full of Trout. There is the Foundation of St. Croix about half a mile in the fields...We have a Collegiate School, a Roman catholic School; a chapel ditto and a Nunnery...*And what improves it all is, the fashionable inhabitants are all gone to Southampton. We are quiet.*"

- John Keats to his sister Fanny. August 28, 1819.

John Keats spent time in Winchester in 1819; his most productive year as a poet. In his letters to friends and family, he often described his affection for the city, and so many of his 'recommendations' still hold true here today. From the Roman roads and Gothic grandeur, to the 'fresh-looking country' where the air is worth 'sixpence a pint' – two hundred years on and this city still remains, a very special one.

But contrary to what the travel guides might tell you, there is more to this city than chalk hills and history. While the air remains fresh, and the churches still stand – industry has blossomed here and those 'fashionable inhabitants' have returned. For this is a newly established centre, for the finest food and world-class sparkling wines, as well as an experimental home for gin. It is a city of coffee roasters and sourdough bakers, Nepalese food and cocktail-makers. We grow watercress, harvest grapes – brew special beer and drink it in special places – and it is equally as worthy of note. So welcome to Winchester, and our introduction to its 'business.' It's a city re-imagined – and a city we are happy to call home.

WINCHESTER LOCATIONS

1   Carter Marsh & Co
2   Magpie Shoe Repairs
3   Jeremy France Jewellers
4   Chesil Theatre
5   Kingsgate Wines & Provisions
6   P&G Wells
7   Hayward Guitars
8   The Hambledon
9   The Consortium
10   Sass & Edge
11   Eclectic Hound
12   Catkin & Pussywillow
13   Cupboard of Health
14   Char Teas
15   Dinghams
16   Old Fashioned Sweetie Shop
17   Wine Utopia
18   Toscanaccio
19   The Winchester Bookshop
20   Projects Emporium
21   Elephant Records
22   The Cheese Stall
23   Hoxton Bakehouse
24   Josie's
25   Rawberry
26   The Winchester Orangery
27   The Dispensary Kitchen
28   Forte Kitchen
29   Flat Whites
30   Beans & Boards
31   Bento Factory
32   Cabinet Rooms
33   Open House Deli
34   Asian Food Hall
35   The Wykeham Arms
36   The Black Boy
37   The Hyde Tavern
38   The Old Vine
39   The Green Man
40   St James Tavern
41   The Westgate
42   Overdraft
43   Greens Bar & Kitchen
44   Incognito
45   The Black Bottle
46   The Chesil Rectory
47   Bridge Street House
48   The Black Rat
49   Tanoshii Fusion
50   Gurkha's Inn
51   Pi Pizza
52   Tom's Deli
53   Kyoto Kitchen
54   Evensong
55   The Minster Gallery
56   The Railway Inn
57   Theatre Royal
58   The Colour Factory
59   Winchester Life Drawing Club
60   Alfred's Brewery
61   Red Cat Brewing

HAMPSHIRE LOCATIONS

River Coffee
Moon Roast Coffee
Gorilla Spirits
Winchester Distillery
The Watercress Company
The Flower Pots Brewery
Hambledon Vineyard
Hattingley Valley Wines
The Wasabi Company

HERITAGE

Carter Marsh & Co

cartermarsh.com
@cartermarshwatches

Carter Marsh & Co was established in 1947 at 32A The Square and has been a magnet for horological collectors and enthusiasts for more than 70 years. The company's showroom reflects the rich history of timekeeping over the past four centuries and has a continually changing selection of the very finest clocks and watches. "I suspect that our longevity is based on hard work, long hours and a real love of horology," company director Darrell Dipper explains. "On my first day back in May 1980, I thought that this is something I would like to do for the rest of my life, and I have often thought that it is the best job in the world." Darrell started working at Carter Marsh & Co, aged 15, as a clockmaker's apprentice and like so many of the company's employees, he has gone on to develop a deep and skilled understanding of all aspects of timekeeping. The company is now a world authority in its field and houses one of the finest horological workshops in the country, offering a full spectrum of services from routine examination to complete restoration.

Magpie Shoe Repairs

5 St Thomas St
SO23 9HE

As you wander along St Thomas Street, you will notice a small handwritten sign to your left that simply reads, 'Shoe Repairs'. The inside is almost completely hidden by a folding wooden screen, but through the narrow-arched doorway, there has been a busy cobbler's workshop for more than 30 years.

Self-promotion is not important to Ray Ballard, the charming owner of Magpie Shoe Repairs. And why would it be? Ray's value to this community is clear – he is the last independent cobbler in Winchester and has been for some time. Ray began working as an apprentice at Shoe Craft on the city's High Street in 1966. It was a time when apprenticeships lasted years rather than months, and it was not until 1971 that he was considered qualified. Today, 54 years later, and in a city centre saturated with 'High Street' competition, he continues to flourish. "They can't get rid of me", Ray jokes. They never will, I thought – since how could anyone compare?

Jeremy France Jewellers

jeremyfrancejewellers.co.uk
@jeremyfrancejewellers

This year marks the 30th anniversary of Jeremy France Jewellers in Winchester. Jeremy's progression into the jewellery trade was one of complete chance – as a baby, he suffered a rather unfortunate accident with a set of Christmas lights, with the resulting electric shock causing his young index finger to distort. Little did he know that years later he would mistakenly attend a silversmithing course at college, where his crooked finger would allow him to work with superior speed and precision to all of his classmates. And the rest, as they say, is history.

After moving to Winchester in 1990, Jeremy worked at the bench by himself as a goldsmith, but his company soon grew, and now employs twenty talented individuals whose skills range from repair and restoration to jewellery design and manufacturing. Jeremey retired at the end of 2018, after 40 years as a goldsmith, but the jewellers continues to thrive as a family-owned business under the direction of his children, Harriet and Christopher France.

Chesil Theatre

chesiltheatre.org.uk
@chesiltheatre

Welcome through the 'Little Red Door' to Chesil Theatre, home of the Winchester Dramatic Society, which has been providing entertainment to the city since 1863. Their dramatic programme runs year-round with the intimate 75-seat studio-style theatre providing a versatile performance space for six productions a year, as well as regularly welcoming professional touring shows, hosted readings, technical training courses, and writing workshops. The theatre itself occupies the former St Peter's Church, which dates in its oldest part from the 12th century, and has made creative use of the available space, as the tower is now a wardrobe and props store, the vestry a dressing room, and the nave and chancel form a flexible auditorium. Chesil Theatre Development Scheme plans to include a new annexe adjacent to the medieval theatre which will create space for a community room, rehearsal space and full facilities for people with disabilities.

Kingsgate Wines & Provisions

kingsgatewineswinchester.co.uk
2-4 Kingsgate St, SO23 9PD

Nestled among the quiet collegiate streets of Kingsgate Village is Kingsgate Wines and Provisions, a general store and fine wine merchant. The premises at 2-4 Kingsgate Street was originally opened as a post office in 1848, and later briefly housed Henry Gunner, a straw hat and bonnet maker for King Edward VII. Then, much to the delight of the locals, it was reopened as a provisions store 23 years ago, and in the following years, over two million pairs of feet have crossed the threshold. As the only grocer south of the cathedral, the traditional village store offers the many local residents a valuable option for fresh milk, locally baked bread, meats, cheese and wine. You will also find fresh flowers guarding the door each day, as well as local Moon Roast Coffee, Hattingley Valley Wines and gins from the Winchester Distillery and Gorilla Spirits. The nearby College students and teachers also share a great affection for the shop, as you will see by the distinct absence of buns and bakery goods after the final ring of the lunch bell.

P&G Wells

bookwells.co.uk
11 College St, SO23 9LZ

Only two minutes walk from Cathedral Close is Britain's oldest independently owned bookshop, P&G Wells. Shop records show that the Austen family bought books here in 1817 when Jane and her sister lived only three doors down on College Walk. The shop was originally opened decades before that by John and Thomas Burden, who supplied stationery and books to the neighbouring pupils of Winchester College. Now two hundred years on, you will still find students shuttling across the shop's many creaking floorboards, among readers of all ages, who gather to appreciate one of the finest bookshops in the country. The bookshelves and tables are elegant and well-stocked, and the window displays change weekly. If you cannot find what you are looking for, the staff will try to order it in. The shop also regularly hosts writing workshops, local reading groups, book launches, as well as 'Storytime' for young children on Wednesday and Saturday mornings.

Hayward Guitars

haywardguitars.com
38 Stockbridge Rd, SO23 7BZ

"When I was 18 years old, I desperately wanted a custom-built guitar. So, I went to see a guitar maker in Cornwall called Kiff Wood – but instead of making one for me – he encouraged me to build my own instead. He gave me a crash course there and then, and sent me off with a pile of wood. I've still got that guitar today."

Hayward Guitars first opened its doors on Stockbridge Road in 2000. Brian Hayward, the shop's owner, has been building and repairing guitars in Winchester for more than 30 years and the respect he has garnered over that time is reflected in the exhaustive line of instruments stacked neatly waiting for repair in his city-centre workshop. As an apprentice, he learned his trade at Whitwams Music Store which used to be on the High Street, before opening his workshop near the station. Brian is a fine example of independent craftsmanship and has truly exceptional skill in his field. So whatever shape, size, age or state of disrepair – your instrument will be in very capable hands.

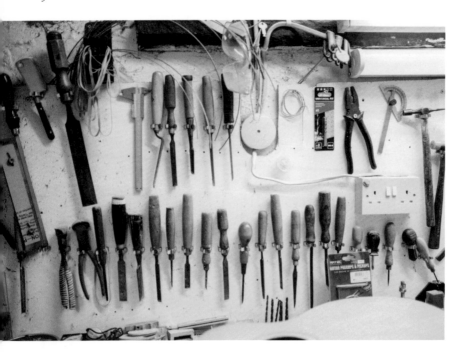

SHOPPING

The Hambledon

thehambledon.com
@thehambledon

After being introduced to shopkeeping by her mother almost from birth, the retail life was perhaps an inevitable one for Victoria Suffield, owner of The Hambledon. "I have a shop because my mum had a shop. She is fantastic. She took me to work when I was six weeks old and left me to sleep under the counter and I suppose that experience seeps into your psyche." A few years later, after spending time working in her mother's shop, Victoria made her own move into the shopkeeping world, opening The Hambledon, in 1999. "I always wanted to create a shop which sold the things I loved, in a space I loved, to people I could grow to love. It's a sentimental kind of aspiration but born out of a genuine love of retail." The distinctive store is much-loved by locals and stocks a carefully curated range of independent brands across multiple departments from lifestyle, homewares and books to women's fashion and menswear. Last year The Hambledon celebrated its 20th birthday by launching exclusive collaborations with some of their favourite brands including Carhartt, Pyrus and Falcon.

The Consortium

theconsortiumonline.co.uk
@the.consortium

The Consortium first opened its doors in 1991 in Romsey. It was a collective approach to tackling a difficult High Street environment whereby local and like-minded crafts dealers came together to create a consortium of vintage and antique goods. The shop soon blossomed into an Aladdin's cave of treasures and expanded to nearby Winchester, where it now occupies 39 Jewry Street. The nine different rooms set over three floors sell everything you could imagine to furnish your home as well as smaller gifts and jewellery. Dressers, trunks, antique mannequins and vintage ice skates can be found alongside Peruvian rugs, Annie Sloan Chalk Paints, and birthday cards in this interesting and eclectic shop.

Sass & Edge

sassandedge.com
@sassandedge

Sass & Edge is an independent womenswear boutique based in the heart of Winchester. Co-founded by friends Sally Gott and Rachel Hunt, Sass & Edge offers a range of smart, casual and stylish pieces from brands around the world. Rachel and Sally are two ladies who share a love of fashion and have extensive experience within the industry. They opened their shop in 2017 to reflect their personalities and to introduce locals to interesting new brands. "We truly do believe that customers love to support their local independents, but we need to give them everything and more than a high street chain or internet company could give. This is where personalised service and those extra touches come in. So we are happy to go to great lengths to source smaller designer brands from countries around the world, so our customer is getting something different." Whether you are popping in for a browse, or in need of some styling advice, the friendly team is on hand to help you get the most out of your shopping experience.

Eclectic Hound

vinetagehound.co.uk
@eclectichound

"We take pride in creating a stimulating place to shop. It's our passion. You can come in looking for a silk shirt and leave with a travel case and a vintage oil candle. Expect the unexpected – we welcome people to just come in and discover something." James and Alice Duffield started selling vintage clothing at Winchester Art and Design Market before opening Vintage Hound in Southgate Street and most recently Eclectic Hound – which opened in The Square in 2017. Eclectic Hound is an independent outfitter stocking men's and ladies apparel, homewares, antiques and oddities. The beautifully curated and interesting store features clothing from established British heritage brands such as Tootal and Catherine Aitken, alongside interesting and unique items from the likes of Elvis & Kresse. You can also find Harris Tweed three-piece suits together with exclusive hand-sewn bow ties and pocket squares that are made right here in the city.

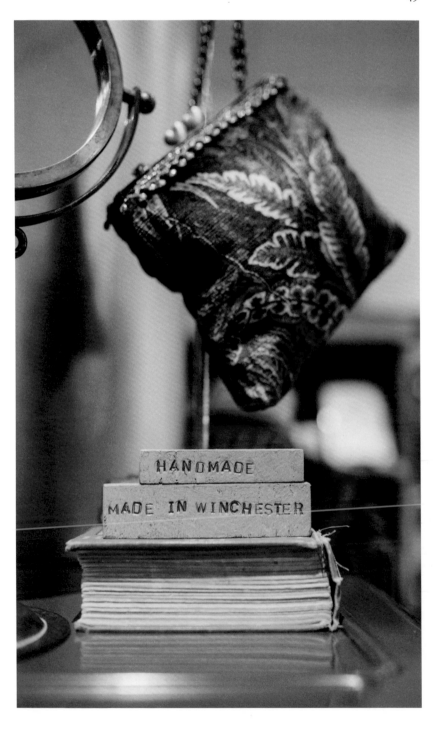

Catkin & Pussywillow

catkinandpussywillow.com
@bloomsdonebeautifully

Ellie Marlow was destined to be a florist. She grew up in the New Forest surrounded by nature and artistry. From snowdrops on mossy banks to narcissi-lined church paths, she was as much delighted by the fine colours and combination of flowers on her doorstep, as by her mother's many depictions of them on canvas. It was perhaps no surprise then, that she chose to leave behind a career in commercial design, for one in horticultural construction. Fond memories of her rural upbringing, now married to a knowledge of fundamental design principles, equals Catkin and Pussywillow, the city's most beloved floristry. Since 2011, her Station Road storefront, together with many workshops and flower schools, have allowed Ellie to share her deep understanding of horticultural artistry. And alongside her small and talented team, she showcases the seasonally changing interplay of textures, colours and scents, both in individual bouquets and larger arrangements. Throughout 2019 and 2020 she will also be hosting a series of workshops covering all aspects of floristry.

Cupboard of Health

facebook.com/
cupboardofhealth

Cupboard of Health is Winchester's only independent health goods store and is committed to stocking only natural, non-synthetic food products and supplementation. The shop also sells a variety of ethical cosmetics, cleansing products and general household items as well as offering the services of a registered nutritional therapist by appointment. Cupboard of Health is an approved stockist of Solgar, Viridian, Wild Nutrition and Dr Hauschka.

Char Teas

charteas.com
@char_teas

Char Teas opened its doors to tea lovers in August 2006 and sells the very best teas from China, India, and around the World. They currently offer a range of over 150 high-quality teas, including the popular 'Lady Winchester' and cherry blossom infused Sencha Sakura from Japan. You will find their teas being used across the city in The Chesil Rectory, The Winchester Orangery and The Wykeham Arms.

Dinghams

dinghams.co.uk
@dinghamscookshop

Old Fashioned Sweetie Shop

oldfashionedsweetieshop.co.uk
@oldfashionedsweetieshop

Inspiring cooks and homemakers everywhere, Dinghams is an independent, family-run, cookshop that offers a large collection of kitchenware, specialising in cooking, baking and tableware, as well as stocking practical ideas for the home. Dinghams first opened its doors in nearby Salisbury, before expansion in 1993 brought the popular homewares business to The Square in Winchester - where it has been a local favourite ever since.

Owner Judith Burnett used to work on a Winchester Market stall before making the move to her High Street candyland ten years ago. As well as countless jars of traditional confectionery, Judith stocks a variety of sugar-free, gluten-free, vegetarian and vegan options for those with different nutritional needs. She also stocks the local Jude's Ice Cream from a small company just two miles down the road in Twyford.

Wine Utopia

wineutopia.co.uk
@wineutopia

Wine Utopia is a locally owned, specialist wine merchant on St Thomas Street. They stock a wide variety of wines from across the world, as well as running both free and tutored tasting events by local and international producers. The store maintains close relationships with Exton Park, Hattingley Valley and Danebury vineyards here in Hampshire, while also hosting exclusive evenings with renowned global vendors and growers including Armit Wines and Chateau Musar. The impressive collection of knowledge possessed by all of the store's qualified experts is also shared throughout the local community, as the shop curates several seasonal wine lists for local businesses like the Greyhound on the Test Hotel and Grosvenor Hotel in Stockbridge, as well as supplying the immensely popular Incognito cocktail bar and The Dispensary Kitchen, here in Winchester.

Toscanaccio

toscanaccio.co.uk
@toscanaccio_uk

"As graduation approached...my in-laws suggested I become a wine buyer, as I was clearly enjoying wine and could count!" Cat Brandwood, the owner of Toscanaccio, graduated from university with a mathematics degree with European studies, and with some helpful advice from her 'in-laws' transitioned seamlessly into the wine business. It was while studying in France as part of her degree that her initial interest was sparked, which later developed into a love of Italian wine and those many unpronounceable varieties that she paired so well with the food she loved to cook. After landing a job in the industry, she refined her knowledge over several years, and upon completion of the WSET qualifications, opened Toscanaccio – an independent Italian wine merchant on Parchment Street. As well as a variety of European and world wines, Cat stocks a selection of local beers and spirits, as well as hosting wine tastings every two or three weeks, a variety of book clubs and private events.

The Winchester Bookshop

@winchesterbookshop
10A St George's St, SO23 8BG

"The Winchester Bookshop is definitely one of my favourite places in the city; I could spend hours there. You can go in looking for Charles Dickens and leave 40 minutes later with a 19th-century map of the Lake District. I love it." (Anonymous bookworm.)

Hidden down an unassuming alleyway off St George's Street is The Winchester Book Shop – one of Hampshire's most interesting literary hangouts. Set over three uneven and characterful floors, the shop deals mostly in antiquarian and second-hand books, as well as a variety of prints, pictures and local ephemera. It was opened in 1991 by four local book dealers, who collaborated to create this impressive vintage collection. There are a number of local titles, maps and historical interest pieces, alongside thousands of items spanning the last hundred years. The Winchester Bookshop is truly a destination for all book lovers and well worth a visit since you never know what you might find there. Gift cards are available for purchase.

Projects Boutique Emporium

projectswinchester.co.uk
@projectsstore

"It all started as an indoor jumble sale," jokes Cassi White, owner of Projects Boutique Emporium. Now, only two years later, her 'jumble sale' has turned into a busy independent cafe, retail emporium, and zero-waste provisions store. 'Projects' is home to over thirty independent local traders – almost exclusively from Hampshire – offering a collection of vintage and hand-made gifts, housewares and collectables, as well as housing an increasingly popular 'Project Zero' division, which offers a range of dry goods and home supplies from carbon-neutral, plastic-free and chemical-free suppliers. What started as a project of passion, soon developed into what is now a sustainable approach to shop-keeping. "We have got to the stage where every other sale in the shop is through Project Zero, so we want to extend to fresh produce, fruit and vegetables." 'Projects', alongside their neighbours Open House Deli are now forerunners in the city's progression into sustainable and environmentally conscious retail.

Elephant Records

@elephantrecordshop
8 Kings Walk, SO23 8AF

"The main reason for starting the shop was my passion for music. I wanted there to be somewhere in Winchester that sold the type of music that I love, instead of having to travel to London or shop online." Tucked-away along Kings Walk – just behind Open House Deli – is Elephant Records. Elephant is Winchester's only independent record store and is the first specialist vinyl shop in the city since Venus Records on St George's Street closed in the 1990s. Local owner Alex Brown started the store as a natural extension of his own considerable vinyl collection and now stocks an even greater array of alternative, underground and independent vinyl, as well as some classic sleeves that everyone will know. Alex shares his love of music with Andy Blockley from Winchester HiFi on Jewry Street, who sells speakers and turntable equipment to get the very best sound from his records. Elephant also stocks a range of CDs and music magazines.

The Cheese Stall

thecheesestall.com
@thecheesestall

For 10 years now, Wintonians have sought guidance from the Goodman family at Winchester Market, for they are the city's only *affineurs*. *Affinage* is the ancestral French art of maturing cheese, a demanding process that requires a great deal of time and consideration for different varieties since each cheese must be allowed to transform naturally under strict temperature and humidity controls. The level of affinage is a matter of personal preference, but for experts, there comes a specific point in time when a cheese can be said to have attained optimum ripeness and it is at this point that Ed, and his parents Graham and Jayne, will sell it.

If you would like to learn more about this transformative process, Ed and his family invite you to visit their 'Cheese HQ' in Winnall, only five minutes from the city-centre, where they will show you the difference between a whole cheese bought at 12 months, and the same cheese finished at 15. If you cannot make it up to the showroom, their famous Cheese Stall is at Winchester Market every Wednesday, Friday, and Saturday.

CAFE & DAYTIME

Hoxton Bakehouse

hoxtonbakehouse.com
@hoxton_bakehouse

"So…we had, like, NO money at all. We bought this really, really cheap, second-hand bread oven, and didn't even have enough money to get it delivered, so went to pick it up in our friend's Transit van." There were certainly a lot of unknowns when Florence Hellier and Darren Bland first started baking bread in 2013, but that little broken oven led them to three stores and over 700 loaves a day – just six years later.

Among all of the stresses and strains involved in a new business, one compelling tenet persisted in their minds: to make no-nonsense "damn good" sourdough bread. So they bought the best local flour from Winchester Mill and got to work hand-crafting each loaf, coaxing it through the exhaustive 36-hour process from first-ferment to baking. "It's a balancing act between temperature, time, moisture, yeast and bacteria. And it needs to be just right." Today, you will find their bread in restaurants and hotels across the city, as well as in their store on Jewry Street where you can pick up a loaf of the finest sourdough and an apple and pecan escargot.

Josie's

josieswinecoffee.com
@josiesuk

In 2017, the Independent newspaper wrote that 'Winchester is not a town famed for its brunch scene' - well, Josie's has since changed that. Alongside the likes of Rawberry, The Winchester Orangery and The Dispensary Kitchen, the city has become a haven for the local day-dwellers who choose to eat between sunup and sundown. This city is now blessed with healthy choices, vegan, vegetarian and carnivorous choices...and then there is Josie's.

Josie's is a delicious nod to the kind of American all-day breakfast spots that offer anything from organic spiced mulberry granola to Mars Bar pancakes. The menu is available all day and is accompanied by locally roasted coffee and juices in the morning, and wine and beer later on. Josie's is the younger sister to the company's first-born which was opened in nearby Bishop's Waltham in 2011 by mother and son team Josephine (Josie) and Kevin Latouf. The brand has since flourished and continues to grow as a family-run independent business, much to the delight of locals.

Rawberry

rawberry.net
@rawberryjuice

"Family, family, family. It's all about family for us," laughs Molly, one-fifth of the true family affair that is Rawberry – Winchester's favourite health food cafe. It was a business that started as it meant to go on – a collaborative effort between family members promoting a shared passion: health. Warren and his son Tom focused on the start-up intricacies and website, while 'Mrs Rawberry', Cheryl, looked after design, ordering and accounts. Which left daughter Molly as general manager, and Emily as head chef, who continues to make all the food fresh, daily.

When their idea came to market, Winchester was a very different place, with very different options. There were no smoothie bars, or health-conscious cafes, no green juices or oat milk. So they decided to go 'all-in' and create a vegetarian juice bar with dairy and gluten-free options on everything. Fast forward to 2020, and they continue to set the nutritional bar in Winchester – from acai bowls and charcoal lattes to bagels and banana bread – Rawberry will be able to satisfy all of your dietary desires.

The Winchester Orangery

thewinchesterorangery.com
@thewinchesterorganery

The Winchester Orangery is one of the city's most recent additions and has instantly become one of the most popular. The vibrant interior, excellent coffee and interesting menus have captured the attention of locals, and are the product of a young team led by general manager Layla Lloyd. "We just wanted to create a functional, beautiful environment for people, and a place where people would be excited to sit down."

In addition to the distinctive ivy-covered walls and leaf-littered ceilings, the Orangery has become well-known for its food and drink. Head of Coffee Ben Lewis, works closely with local artisan roasters 'River Coffee' who use only the best specialty beans. And in the kitchen, the creative team is delivering constantly changing daytime and evening menus, offering anything from grilled halloumi flatbread with pickled cucumber and harissa mayonnaise – to red wine-glazed venison, with juniper dust and beetroot. All of the dishes are available alongside a full wine and cocktail menu.

The Dispensary Kitchen

@thedispensarykitchen
5-6 The Square, SO23 9ES

Aiden and Vanity met on New Zealand's South Island and share a love for the Antipodean way of cooking. As a native Australian, Vanity grew up in the kitchens of Perth and Brisbane, where the daytime fare is a relaxed and informal celebration of vibrant and diverse ingredients. They opened The Dispensary Kitchen in 2017 as a celebration of that experience, and to create an environment for people who want to have breakfast at 2 pm, and for those who want to enjoy something just a little bit outside of the traditional British culinary experience.

Offering jalapeno and bacon waffles as well as coconut and cherry porridge with maple syrup and passionfruit – the team is constantly innovating. The specials change daily depending on what ingredients become available and everything is made on-site, from paprika hollandaise, to their lavender-infused honey. Even the excess syrup from the poached rhubarb granola gets used to create rhubarb and gin Bellini's. Breakfast and lunch are served all day, together with a full wine, beer and cocktail list.

Forte Kitchen

fortekitchen.co.uk
@forte_kitchen

Flat Whites

@flatwhitescoffee
Market Ln, SO23 9EP

Forte Kitchen in Parchment Street is a daytime dining hall that combines the good food of a fine dining experience with the more informal and relaxed environment of traditional cafe culture. It was opened in 2014 by Winchester locals Naomi Beamish and Olly Biggs who have combined their favourite aspects of daytime and evening dining to produce a menu of simple food, executed perfectly.

Flat Whites' is Winchester's favourite takeaway coffee stop, providing artisanal coffee, Char Teas and a healthy selection of sandwiches, light bites and cakes. The distinctive mobile pod on Market Street is now accompanied by a second, sister shop, in Stonemason's Court on Parchment Street, for those wanting a more leisurely sit-down experience.

Beans & Boards

beansandboards.co.uk
@beansandboards

Bento Factory

@bentofactoryco
1 St Thomas St, SO23 9HE

Jack Vear started Beans and Boards in June 2016 after growing up in Winchester's skateboarding community. His small independent skate store-cum-coffee shop serves a vibrant local youth community from neighbouring Peter Symonds College, The Westgate School and Kings' School. He also stocks a variety of clothing, apparel and art from local brands Passim from Southampton, and Simply Boy by Winchester local Jon James.

The Bento Factory is Winchester's newest micro-eatery, offering Japanese and Korean inspired breakfast and lunch dishes, as well as a range of daily specials, curries and soups. A number of meat, fish and vegetable options are always available in addition to some traditional British and East Asian desserts, Vietnamese coffee and a range of teas.

Cabinet Rooms

cabinetrooms.com
@cabinetrooms

Gary and Marcus opened Cabinet Rooms in 2014, as a safe and relaxing environment in which to enjoy great food, drink, music and film. In the beautifully presented downstairs 'cabinet rooms' they regularly host book clubs, writing workshops and film screenings with the main ground floor space functioning as a perpetual and quite Parisian, cafe-bar. There are stylish references throughout to the famous Charleston House which provided refuge and inspiration to the Bloomsbury Group, as well as the unmistakable influence of the *Restoration* period cafe spaces in which you could meet friends, drink coffee, read books and discuss politics. Cabinet Rooms functions perfectly – as Mariana Starke wrote of those early 19th century cafes – as 'a place where tea, coffee, chocolate, etc. are served in the morning; and coffee, liqueurs, beer...and ices in the evening' – at Cabinet Rooms you will find all of the above. The finest English tea and artisan coffee, alongside local spirits and Hampshire sparkling wines, cakes from Hoxton Bakehouse and homemade Portuguese tarts.

Open House Deli

openhousedeli.co.uk
@openhousedeli

When Rebecca Smith started trading at Winchester Market she soon realised that there was a real appetite for her concept of sustainable daytime dining. "I want customers to feel assured when they are buying from us, they can be sure we have thought about their food, where it has come from and what ingredients are included – we are as transparent as possible with our supply chain." Open House is now one of the city's most sustainable businesses and has successfully implemented that ethos across every aspect of their store. They buy the majority of their dry goods in 25kg recyclable sacks, and select suppliers based on their use of plastics and food miles. They consciously decide to not serve certain ingredients because of their farming practises or shipping methods and they make everything from scratch – cakes, salads, soups, hot pots – not even stocks, jars of sauce or pastes are bought in. "We know exactly every ingredient in our food and where it has come from," and the results are delicious. You can also find a host of natural and plastic-free items in the small, well-stocked retail space.

Asian Food Hall

51 Upper Brook St
SO23 8DG

The Asian Food Hall (formerly Chinatown) is a small family-run supermarket and canteen. As you walk through the front sliding doors, to the left is a small grocery store, with three well-stocked aisles of Asian spices, sauces and dry goods, as well as fresh vegetables and frozen meat. The store specialises in Chinese and South-East Asian produce, but you will regularly find Japanese, Korean and Middle-Eastern staples lining the colourful shelves.

On the other side of the shop, to the right, is a small Asian food hall, where the food is excellent. General unfamiliarity with the store means that it is often overlooked as a culinary destination – but if you peer through the little red hatch at the very end of the dining room, you will find a busy kitchen producing reasonably priced authentic, street-style dishes from all over South East Asia. It is a quick and easy destination for delicious dishes such as Vietnamese Pho, wonton dumpling soup, bbq lemongrass pork and stir-fried noodles.

PUBS & BARS

The Wykeham Arms

wykehamarmswinchester.co.uk
@thewykeham

This famous city corner-house has been a hostelry since 1755, when it offered rest and refreshment to those travelling to and from the south coast. Lord Nelson is said to have been one such roomer, who used the inn on his journeys to Portsmouth. Today, the pub owes most of its fame and affection to former landlord Graeme Jameson, who transformed The Wykeham Arms into one of the city's most beloved landmarks. Under his management, the pub blossomed into a vibrant community hub, filled with locals from the nearby College and Cathedral who admired both his spirit and generosity. In the early '90s when Winchester Cathedral was raising money for the endowment of its choral foundation, Graeme helped to raise £60,000 to secure the salaries of lay clerk singers, and developed a lasting bond with the Cathedral, whose choir still return regularly for a drink after Evensong. Sadly, Graeme passed away in the summer of 2002, but his legacy remains in his remarkable collection of bar tankards, school canes and local ephemera, which still decorate the pub's walls today.

The Black Boy

theblackboypub.com
1 Wharf Hill, SO23 9NP

The Black Boy is another iconic Winchester pub. This traditional backstreet alehouse, tucked away on Wharf Hill, is highly regarded by locals and offers an unparalleled eclectic drinking experience. The pub's five rooms are arranged around the central bar, each very different, and each a hoarder's museum. Ranks of antique fire buckets hang above a stuffed donkey, cradling an equally stuffed baboon in one corner, whilst another displays a thousand green bottles and a taxidermied giraffe. "I wanted something for people to look at," says the pub landlord David Nicholson. "If you're waiting at the bar for a friend on your own, you don't look a complete fool." Well, there is plenty to look at – I can assure you – in what is now one of the city's most interesting and famous landmarks.

The Hyde Tavern

hydetavern.co.uk
57 Hyde St, SO23 7DY

In the 18th century, Hyde Street was well populated by inns and forges, but today there is one pub that stands in charming isolation. As you stoop through the narrow front doors of The Hyde Tavern, it will not surprise you to know that the beams above your head have long-since celebrated their 500th birthday. The building is understood to have been a functioning coaching-inn since 1700 when horses would be stabled in what is now the tavern's cellar, and then a public house since 1867, with no break in tenancy. It is a staggering tenure that reflects the Hyde's value not only as a local drinking hole, but also as a vibrant community hub that regularly holds live music and literary workshops, folk practices and knitting groups. It is a place that does not serve food, but you are welcome to pay £1 for a plate, knife and fork from the bar and enjoy whatever culinary delight you can arrange to be delivered to the door. Expect warm hospitality and local ales from Flower Pots, Alfred's Brewery and Red Cat, in one of Winchester's finest pubs.

The Old Vine

oldvinewinchester.com
@oldvinewinch

The Old Vine is a beautiful eighteenth-century pub in the very centre of Winchester. In the summer months, you can enjoy a drink on one of the outside tables overlooking the Cathedral grounds, or sit inside the characterful Grade II listed inn. The menu offers a constantly changing insight into local Hampshire producers, from Cottonworth sparkling wines to beers by Andwell Brewing Company and Red Cat.

The Green Man

greenmanwinchester.pub
@thegreenman_winch

Only a couple of minutes walk from the High Street is The Green Man – an attractive city-centre pub and dining room, serving local ales from Alfred's Brewery and The Flower Pots Brewery, as well as a range of cocktails and fine wines. This stylish retro-themed bar is located directly opposite Winchester's beautiful Everyman cinema, offering the perfect location for a drink, before or after a film.

St James Tavern

the.littlepubgroup.co.uk
@stjamestavernwinchester

The Westgate

westgatewinchester.com
@westgate_winchester

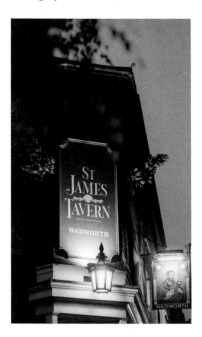 

Just a short walk up Romsey Road is one of the city's most intimate community pubs: St James Tavern. This charming and cosy cornerhouse is set over three uneven floors and plays host to regular live music events and well-attended quiz nights, as well as 'Burger Nights' and 'Pie Nights' every Monday and Wednesday evening. Local options include Silverback Gin from Gorilla Spirits and Danebury Vineyards sparkling wine.

Standing proudly at the top of the High Street and in the heart of the city is The Westgate. It is just a short stroll from the fortified medieval gateway after which it is named and houses a well-stocked bar, dining room and ten individually decorated boutique rooms - all offering beautiful views of the city.

Overdraft

@overdraftbeerandtacos
5 Jewry St, SO23 8RZ

Overdraft Craft Ale Bar was opened in October 2017 by father and son duo Amrik and Mikha Rai. It has a rotating selection of up to 30 local, national and international beers and provides Winchester locals with a unique insight into the world of smaller, craft brewing. The bar hosts regular 'tap-takeovers' – when microbreweries from around the country are invited to sell their entire range on cask and keg; as well as an ongoing 'taste-of' series – where patrons are introduced to the various craft producers of any one British city. Overdraft also houses an increasingly popular street food canteen which cooks fresh, Mexican-American finger food, all made from scratch on-site – from Matcha Chicken Wings to the Poblano Carnitas Tacos. The Overdraft team took their love of craft beer one step further in 2019, by teaming up with Unity Brewery in Southampton to produce their first branded beer, *Stylus*, a very bright and sessionable golden ale. You can try Stylus on tap today – alongside any of the beers on offer – as a pint, half-pint, tasting flight, or to take-away.

Greens Bar & Kitchen

greensbarandkitchen.co.uk
@greens_bar_

"Greens is a bit like Cheers - it is a place where everybody knows your name, and everyone is welcomed into the party. It is a unique place." General manager Liz Dear started working at Greens as a student in 1999 while studying at the University of Winchester, and like many locals, has fallen in love with the popular venue. "The atmosphere is key. We are friendly, welcoming and conscientious without being pretentious or arrogant, and as a result, it is a place that means a lot to many people." Greens Bar & Kitchen has been a Winchester institution for 30 years now, after it was opened in 1989 by Peter Neave and his wife Liz. The busy kitchen serves breakfast and lunch every day of the week, but Greens truly comes alive in the evenings and at the weekends when many locals flock to the bar for some of the best cocktails in the city. Signature drinks include the passion fruit, mango and lemon martini, the rhubarb and gin sour, and a host of bespoke specials like the lemongrass and mezcal margarita.

Incognito

Incognitowinchester.co.uk
@incognitococktailbars

From hot air balloons complete with clouds, to edible ducks and functioning Ferris wheels: welcome to Incognito, Winchester's favourite cocktail bar. Hidden on the ground floor of the Grade I listed St John's House, Incognito takes the purposefully over-the-top theatrics of 1930's American high-society and injects it with modern mixology to create a multi-sensory experience unavailable anywhere else in the city. The bar's theme is built around the story of its mythical owner Chadwick Smithfield, a globetrotting cat burglar whose plunder adorns every wall of this striking speakeasy bar. Smithfield's story is then told through the creative drinks menus, which offer an insight into the different flavours and regions he has experienced along the way. You'll find interesting new spirits from New York, Jakarta, Marrakech and Paris, as well as innovative and theatrical in-house cocktails like the signature 'Rubber Dub, Dub' - which mixes Bathtub gin with Dolin Blanc Vermouth, Rhubarb, Rose, Raspberry and Yuzu, topped with lavender bubbles and a chocolate duck.

The Black Bottle

theblackbottle.co.uk
@theblackbottlewinch

The Black Bottle is Winchester's first self-service wine bar. Enter through the small and discrete side entrance on Water Lane and you will be handed a dispensing card. From there, load your card and proceed through the narrow doorway and along the creaky floorboards to enjoy a choice of over 32 bottles from a 140-bottle strong cellar, all of which are perfectly preserved and delivered through Enomatic dispensers in either 25ml, 125ml or 175ml measures.

From there, it is easy. Simply wander from room to room, insert the card into the machines and grab a glass. The cellar is well stocked, from Bordeaux to Lebanon, South Australia to India, and knowledge is always on hand to provide context and direction to your experience. Cheese and charcuterie boards are also available and sourced directly from the fresh-food market stalls just metres away on the High Street.

RESTAURANTS

The Chesil Rectory

chesilrectory.co.uk
@chesil_rectory

Whether you are from Winchester or just passing through, you will no doubt recognise the half-timbered two-storey building at the bottom of Chesil Street. The building has an illustrious 600-year-old history and was once owned by Henry VIII, but now continues as Winchester's oldest commercial property - housing one of its very best restaurants. The Grade II listed building provides a charming and stylish backdrop to the creative modern-British cuisine served up by executive chef Damian Brown and head chef James Wills.

Together with owners Mark and Eleanor Dodd, they have created an exceptional display of what Hampshire and the South Coast has to offer. From locally pressed oils and foraged fruit jams, to free-range Greenfield Pork and plaice from the Cornish dayboats – at Chesil Rectory you can expect menus brimming with local produce, served in intimate and historic surroundings.

Bridge Street House

bridgestreethouse.co.uk
@bridgestreet_house

Bridge Street House is one of the newest additions to Winchester's city centre. It opened its doors in the summer of 2019 as a bar and restaurant with a small number of boutique rooms, and within weeks it developed a reputation for classic, elegant cocktails and inventive, modern British fine dining. The small dining room seats 34 people and provides an intimate and engaging experience as the chefs make everything right in front of you from the open-plan kitchen. Their creative, seasonal menus showcase the many local artisan producers and growers right here in Hampshire, and under the direction of head chef Stuart Dawkins, the kitchen often utilise the abundance of local game, fresh-water fish, foraged fungi and herbs as well as daily deliveries of organic bread from the sustainable microbakery '108 The Bakery', in Romsey. "We only want to use the freshest, local produce, and we're happy to change the menu every week if something amazing comes through the door." The highly regarded food is complemented by seasonal wine and cocktail lists curated by bar manager Evangelos Balasas.

The Black Rat

theblackrat.co.uk
88 Chesil St, SO23 0HX

Formerly a pub, The Black Rat transformed in 2007 into a quiet, innovative restaurant and just one year after opening its doors was awarded a Michelin star. Modern British fare with a distinct European bent is the restaurant's speciality, with a constantly evolving menu set within its quirky bohemian interior. Jon Marsden-Jones and his team consistently prepare refined, British dishes which showcase much of Hampshire's vibrant produce as well as all that they have personally grown in the restaurant's nearby allotments. Expect creative local dishes like the beetroot-cured Chalkstream trout with wasabi, Granny Smith apple and pickled clams. Or veal loin with sweetbreads and bone marrow pommes anna. Complement the meals with a selection from the outstanding wine list and coffee from local artisan roasters, Moon Roast.

Tanoshii Fusion

tanoshiifusion.co.uk
12 Upper High St, SO23 8UT

Tanoshii Fusion is a small, family-run restaurant offering a selection of the finest dishes from across East Asia. Inspired by Chinese, Thai, Korean, Japanese and Indonesian flavours - the talented chefs use authentic Asian cooking techniques to deliver an extensive menu which includes Japanese Sushi, Chinese Dim Sum, Korean Bibimbap, Thai and Indonesian curries. Seafood options include monkfish, scallops and soft-shell crab, alongside all of the staple favourites, as well as a variety of meat and vegetarian options. If Asian food is new to you – or there is simply too much choice on the menu – you can choose from three 'set menu' options that provide an introductory mix of dishes from across the region. They also offer a variety of Asian craft beers, plum wines and premium saki, as well as local gins from Winchester Distillery, Gorilla Spirits and Bombay Sapphire.

Gurkha's Inn

gurkhasinnwinchester.com
17 City Rd, SO23 8SD

Chef Tika Ram Niure brings Nepal's interesting and unique cuisine to Winchester. Tika was born and raised in the remote Mt. Dhaulagiri region of northwest Nepal and started his career working in hotels and restaurants across Nepal and India before moving to England and opening 'Gurkha's Inn' in 2014. 'Gurkha's' is now a favourite among Winchester locals and serves both Nepalese and Indian dishes expertly blended to bring out the rich aromas and authentic flavours of these culinarily diverse regions. As the attentive hosts will explain to you, Nepal is home to many different tribal groups and regions, each with their own unique culture and cooking practises and the Gurkha's Inn presents you with a selection of dishes to give you an authentic experience of that.

Pi Pizza

pi-pizza.co.uk
@pipizzauk

Following a transformative period working in a Florence pizzeria, first-time restaurateur Rosie Whaley was inspired to open Pi Pizza. Five years on, and Pi is Winchester's favourite stop for an authentic Italian slice. The popular 20-inch sharing pizzas (also available in 12"), are the product of a creative team of only Sicilian chefs, whose 72-hour dough fermentation process results in the lightest lean bases authentic to home. Every ball of dough is made in-house from Italian flour and stretched to order by hand right in front of you.

Everything else is a mix of the best Italian and English ingredients. Charcuterie produce comes only from the finest producers in South Tyrol, Calabria and Parma in Italy, with all other meats from Hampshire farms. You will find the creamiest whole Italian mozzarella balls from Italy, alongside cheeses from Lyburn Farm in the New Forest which provides the famous 'Old Winchester' for the cauliflower cheese pizza. Even the sorbet and gelato are handmade to order by local friends Mooka, in Petersfield.

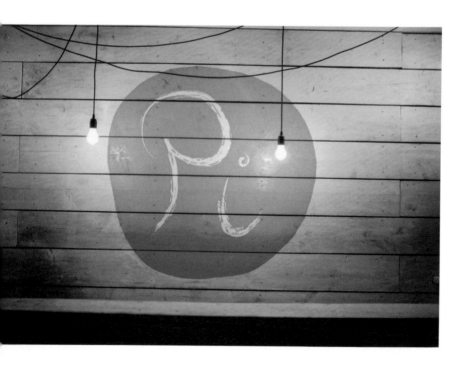

Tom's Deli

tomsdeli.co.uk
@toms_deli

When Tommaso Romita took over a small city-centre newsagent in 1987, he complained to his cousins in Puglia about how business was slow, so they began sending over family-made oils, preserves and pastries from his home in Puglia, Italy. Realising that the locals had an appetite for Italian produce, Tommaso continued to add more and more items including home-made tortellini, lasagne and tiramisu, and soon enough, the small newsagent had blossomed into Tom's Deli. Schiraldi olive oil, lemon biscuits, and other esoteric foods like baccalà (salt cod) and Sicilian lemons soon followed, as did the addition of a coffee machine and outside seating. Now more than 30 years later and Tom's Deli is a small and immensely popular family-run Italian restaurant that offers authentic Italian dishes like seafood linguine, spaghetti with meat sauce, and homemade cannoli.

Kyoto Kitchen

kyotokitchen.co.uk
@kyotokitchen

Head chef Shunji Irokawa trained in classical Japanese cooking in 1972 – where he grew up just north of Tokyo. Shunji moved to the UK over 20 years ago, and brings with him the essence of Japanese dining to Kyoto Kitchen on Parchment Street.

Together with owner Miff Kayum, Shunji has created a mix of traditional and modern authentic dishes that manage to utilise the finest local ingredients that suit the style so well. Kyoto's signature dish is the Winchester Roll, which uses the leaves of locally grown wasabi to wrap hot-smoked trout from chalk stream rivers only five miles away. The fresh wasabi root is then grated at the table to ensure the release of a much sweeter and more refined flavour. The menu also boasts a variety of small plates, tempura, sashimi and rolls, all accompanied by a diverse drinks menu, curated specifically for their food by local masters of wine Peter Richards and Susie Barrie, which includes seven varieties of still and sparkling sake, in addition to local sparkling wine from Hambledon Vineyard.

THE ARTS

Evensong

Winchester Cathedral
9 The Close, SO23 9LS

Choral Evensong is one of the glories of British musical tradition, and is free of charge and open to all. It is a 45-minute church service in which the 'song' of voices is heard at the 'even' point between the active day and restful night. As an English language service, Evensong dates back to the time of the Reformation, with the liturgy – that the Church uses to this day – first laid out in Archbishop Cranmer's Book of Common Prayer, in 1549.

Six nights a week, at 5.30 pm, and Sundays at 3.30 pm, Winchester Cathedral is filled with the sound of the Cathedral choir. The service begins with a short prayer sung by the cantor and the choir, and is followed by readings from the Bible, further prayer and more choral performances. The long-established and internationally acclaimed Winchester Cathedral Choir includes 22 boy choristers and 12 adult lay clerk singers who also perform regularly in media recordings, broadcasts, concerts and international tours. This 500-year-old choral music tradition is simply unmissable.

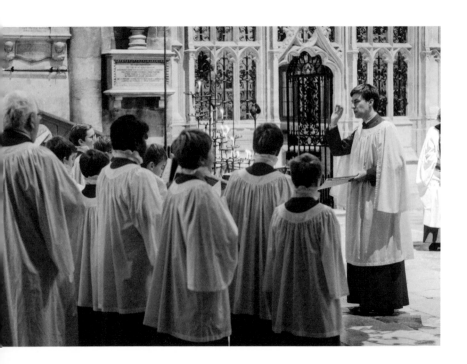

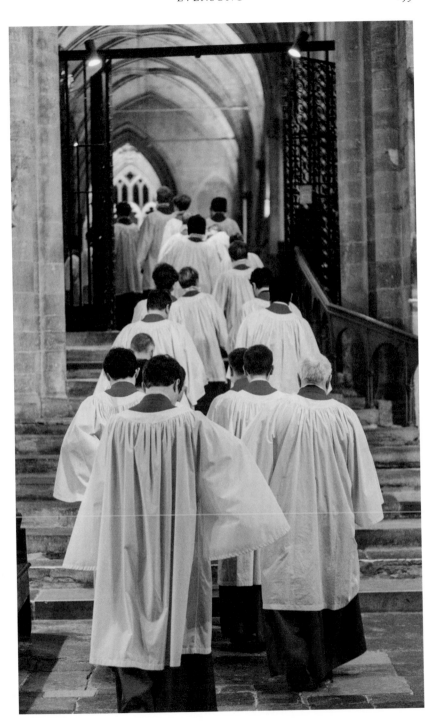

The Minster Gallery

minstergallery.com
@theminstergallery

Ines Graham opened The Minster Gallery in 2010, in the former residence of the poet John Keats at 3A Minster Street, Winchester. Art has been in Ines' family blood for years. Her grandmother worked for the Musée du Louvre in Paris after the Second World War before her mother became an art critic. The Minster Gallery, overlooking the cathedral, has three rooms displaying an extensive selection of works by many well established and emerging artists, both British and international. As well as a continuously changing display of work by core artists such as Patrick Gibbs, Jean Noble, Netta Carey, and Andrew Stock. Ines also specialises in curating fine art for private collectors, corporate clients and interior designers, as well as sourcing commissions and loaned pieces for businesses and private exhibitions.

Sonder

sonderfilms.co
@sonderfilms

Sonder is an independent film production company based in Winchester and London. Local friends Joel Barney, Oscar Ferguson and Ozzi Sanderson started with a desire to make films for fun, but the group's distinctive and striking visual style soon drew the attention of film festivals and local businesses eager to have their brand's story told by the young collective. The company's fast-growing accounts sheet now boasts the likes of Josie's, Overdraft and The Hambledon, as well as globally established brands Bang & Olufsen and The Peligoni Club. In recent months, the group has demonstrated particular skill in the short-film and storytelling formats, working with the internationally acclaimed dancer Mukeni Nel, and local artist Josh Hoffman, with whom they created the visually mesmerising docu-short: 'A Dance with Paint'. Sonder also produced the 20th-anniversary celebration visuals for the much-loved local department store, The Hambledon.

Harvey Gorst

harvgorst.com
@harvgorst

Simeon Leeder

simeonleeder.co.uk
@simeonleeder

Harvey Gorst is a documentary photographer and visual storyteller from Winchester. He is currently studying photography under the tutelage of international exhibitor Dinu Li at the University of Falmouth. Harvey accepts commissions and specialises in behind the scenes photography for motion pictures and television as well as shooting portraiture and landscape on 35mm film.

Simeon Leeder is a freelance camera operator and photographer from Winchester. He shot and edited the popular Youtube series 'Taste Buds' and is a camera operator on short films and music videos for the Sonder production company. He shoots mainly on film and is available for private commissions and magazine editorials.

Ben Lewis

The Winchester Orangery
@barista_benji

Ben Rowe

Hoxton Bakehouse
@baristaprogress

If you drink coffee in Winchester, there is a good chance that you will know - or get to know - Ben Lewis and Ben Rowe. Ben Lewis, or 'Benji', is a talented barista and Head of Coffee at the popular Winchester Orangery. He has been a finalist in the UK Latte Art Championship for the last two years - and placed second in 2018. You can see his amazing designs in person, every week at The Orangery or online, on his Instagram account.

Ben Rowe, also known as 'Progress', leads the coffee proceedings at Hoxton Bakehouse. He is the host of the 'Filtered Thoughts' podcast: an online discussion show that explores the world of specialty coffee. He is also involved in research and development within the coffee industry for companies like La Marzocco and Victoria Arduino.

The Railway Inn

therailwayinn.pub
@railwaylive

Theatre Royal

theatreroyalwinchester.co.uk
@theatreroyalwinch

The Railway Inn has been the city's home of live music since the late 1970s. It has been an early exploration space for several notable careers, including Dua Lipa, Ed Sheeran, Laura Marling and Frank Turner, as well as providing locals with regular comedy nights, spoken word events and 'Roots' - Winchester's longest-running open mic event, which celebrated its 20th-anniversary in 2018.

The Theatre Royal has been providing Winchester with theatrical entertainment since 1978. It is currently directed by the 'Play to the Crowd' Arts and Education charity that aims to inspire people of all ages to connect with, and participate in, live performance. The theatre hosts regular travelling productions, musical and comedy performances, as well as hosting its own shows and seasonal panto.

Ted Hepenstal

tedhepenstal.com
@tedhepenstalart

The Colour Factory

thecolourfactory.org.uk
@thecolourfactory_winchester

Ted Hepenstal is a Winchester-born artist. His Post-Impressionist style paintings celebrate the distinctive seasonal variation of his home county of Hampshire and portray the rich variety of local panoramas from the bluebell forests at Micheldever to sunsets on St Catherine's Hill. Some of his original work is on display at the Fulflood Gallery in Winchester and seasonally at the Alresford Arts Festival.

The Colour Factory is a collaborative studio space in Winchester housing six resident full-time artists and silversmiths. They offer a variety of engaging classes and educational workshops across all levels, as well as taking an active role in local community projects across Hampshire. You can see their collective works on display around the city, including their famous painted bollards in the Square.

Winchester Life Drawing Club

@winchesterlifedrawingclub
15 Kings Walk, SO23 8AF

"We started a life drawing society at Winchester School of Art in 2018. I was a second-year Fine Arts student, and just wanted to create a place for people to relax, get creative and socialise." Jakob Davies, along with friends and fellow students Amy Murphy and Sam Hanikene, noticed that many of the art classes around Winchester stopped running during the summer months, so wanted to provide a reliable weekly session for enthusiasts to keep attending and to which all members of the community were invited to attend. The sessions became incredibly popular with the public and suddenly Winchester Life Drawing Club was formed. The club now leads two two-hour classes every week, on Tuesday evening and Wednesday lunchtime, at the Nutshell Arts Centre in King's Walk. It caters for all levels and provides equipment and instruction when required.

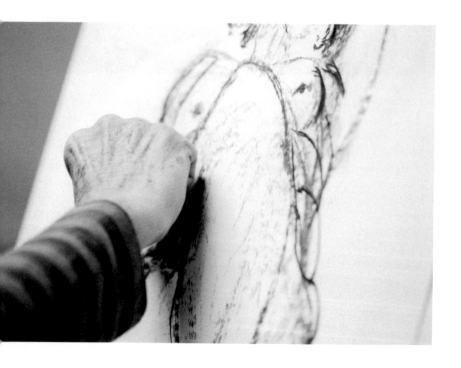

ELKA: Sustainable Textiles

elkatextiles.co.uk
@elka_textiles

ELKA is a woven textile studio based in Winchester, where textile designer Ellie Fisher produces bespoke handwoven textiles for fashion, furnishing, and by commission. After completing a foundation course at Winchester School of Art, Ellie completed a BA in Textile Design and a Master's degree in Design and Textile Futures at the revered Central Saint Martins college of art and design in London. After graduating in 2006, she returned home to Winchester to set up her weaving business in a small city-centre studio – where she has been weaving for 13 years now.

As well as making a range of woven goods, Ellie – along with her mother Claudia – produces naturally dyed yarns and offers a range of weaving and dying workshops. She travels around the South of England teaching group classes, as well as offering half-day and full-day workshops on her Louet Megado loom from her own studio. Ellie is also increasingly known for her recycling of existing textile products like vintage denim and traditional silk kimonos that she imports from Japan.

Jennibloom Floral Design Studio

jennibloom.com
@jennibloomflowers

While working in the financial industry, Jen Prosser started to teach herself the basics of floristry. It was a natural progression from the gardening that she loved to do and in 2014, she left the corporate world behind and started Jennibloom Floral Design Studio in Winchester. Her artistic talent was clear from the beginning and now only five years later, she creates beautiful and intricate displays for up to 20 weddings each year, as well as a range of smaller bespoke commissions and editorials.

"Essentially I like to keep my arrangements as close to their natural form as possible. I like the flowers to express themselves, to dance around and not force them into position. I just try to make the most of their interesting shapes." Her distinctive artistic style has garnered the attention of luxury perfumers Miller Harris and the British clothing brand Joules, with whom she works regularly to create striking store window displays and installations for pop-up events. Jenni also offers private one-to-one tuition for anyone interested in a career in floral design.

LOCAL PRODUCERS

River Coffee

rivercoffeeroasters.com
@rivercoffeeuk

Will Harrigan only started roasting coffee in Winchester 18 months ago, but he has already managed to establish himself as the main supplier to many to the city's most loved coffee-stops. You will find his soft blends and single-origin brews in the likes of Hoxton Bakehouse, Rawberry and The Winchester Orangery, as well as many coffee shops and kitchens across the country.

Will only roasts to order, and he is not afraid to pay premiums for specialty green coffee to ensure the very best results in every roast. He also makes regular visits to South America in order to better understand the processes of production as well as to foster direct relationships with growers. As a way of honouring the skill and labour of the communities from which he sources his beans, Will adds a farmer's name to most of the coffee orders that he ships out of his roastery. From producer to brewer, it is River Coffee's holistic approach to the industry that allows them to produce some of the very finest coffee this country has to offer.

Moon Roast Coffee

moonroast.co.uk
@moonroastcoffee

If you have ever dined at The Chesil Rectory, The Black Rat or Bridge Street House, you will know Francis Bradshaw's coffee. Francis is a fourth-generation producer, who began roasting for himself in 2014, in a small shed at the back of his home. At the time, Francis had a full-time job, so would roast only at night, with very little but the sound of the owls hooting and bright moonlight for company. And hence, Moon Roast was born.

Five years on, and Moon Roast is producing small-batch specialty coffee, as well as providing expert domestic and commercial barista training courses for customers. You are also welcome to visit the roastery and cafe where Francis and his team will walk you through the process of producing coffee; from sampling and cracking, to the finer arts of cupping and blending. If you cannot make it up to the roastery, his coffee is available to purchase in Toscanaccio and Kingsgate Wines and Provisions. You can also try the Gorilla Spirits 'Maraba' coffee liqueur, which is made using Rwandan beans from Moon Roast.

Gorilla Spirits

gorillaspirits.co.uk
@gorillaspirits

"I strongly believe that all businesses should make a positive contribution to the world. This fundamental belief lies at the centre of everything that we do at Gorilla Spirits and of course our contribution to gorilla conservation is a major focus for us." Andy Daniels started Gorilla Spirits back in 2011, retaining a sense of social responsibility at every level of his business, and is proud to donate £1 from every bottle sold, to The Gorilla Organization which is at the forefront of conservation across Africa.

For the Gorilla team, it does not end there. Andy and his staff are investigating the future use of aluminium containers as an environmentally ethical choice to reduce both recycling waste and shipping weights. They also encourage visitors who attend their popular gin schools and cocktail masterclasses to purchase bottles from the local village shop to help ensure their success. In 2019, Andy's efforts were formally recognised, as Gorilla Spirits received an International CSR Excellence Award for their ongoing displays of corporate social responsibility.

Winchester Distillery

winchesterdistillery.co.uk
@winchester_distillery

Just metres from the watercress fields in nearby Old Alresford, is Winchester Distillery, the home of Twisted Nose gin. Paul Bowler started the company back in 2014 from his kitchen in central Winchester and after amazing success, relocated to be next to the chalk stream watercress beds that fragrance his award-winning gins. Yet, the journey to creating what is now the distillery's signature gin, Twisted Nose, was not an easy one. In fact, it was not until recipe number 84 that Paul was satisfied he had achieved what he had set out to make. The ten botanicals, including juniper and locally grown watercress, are distilled slowly to maintain the freshness and delicate aromas and the result is an intense, fragrant and refreshing gin. You can find Twisted Nose and a range of Winchester Distillery spirits across the pubs and bars of Winchester and for sale in Wine Utopia, Toscanaccio and Kingsgate Wines and Provisions.

The Watercress Company

thewatercresscompany.com
@thewatercressco

The Flower Pots Brewery

flowerpotscheriton.co.uk
Cheriton, SO24 0QQ

Watercress has been grown in the United Kingdom for centuries and Hampshire's abundance of pure, mineral-rich chalk streams provide some of the best growing conditions in the country. Only two miles from the centre of Winchester, The Watercress Company has been farming for over 20 years on traditional beds that have commercially produced watercress since 1850.

The Flower Pots Brewery lies in the village of Cheriton, seven miles to the east of Winchester. Brewing began back in 2006, and three regular beers: Perridge Pale, Flowerpots Bitter and Goodens Gold quickly became Hampshire favourites. You will find their popular ale in pubs across the city, including The Wykeham Arms, The Black Boy and The Hyde Tavern.

Alfred's Brewery

alfredsbrewery.co.uk
@alfredsbrewer

Red Cat Brewing

redcatbrewing.co.uk
@redcatbrewing

'Alfred's' is a Winchester microbrewery founded in 2012 by husband and wife Steve and Isabelle Haigh. Their immensely popular 'Saxon Bronze' ale shot to fame in the company's first two years and has since been adopted by pubs and bars all over the city. You can also pick up 'takeaway' beer direct from the brewery every Friday between 4-6 pm.

Andy Mansell and Iain McIntosh started Red Cat Brewing in 2013 with the sole aim of creating imaginative and innovative craft beer. "We wanted to challenge ourselves with different beer styles and processes, learn as much as we can, and innovate." Red Cat now creates a variety of Winchester's favourite beers from session pales and IPAs, to lemon-infused Kairos and coffee cream stout.

Hambledon Vineyard

hambledonvineyard.co.uk
@hambledon_vineyard

Just a 25-minute drive from Winchester, is Hambledon Vineyard – the oldest commercial vineyard in England. It was established in 1952, when Sir Guy Salisbury-Jones planted the very first vines with the help of the distinguished Pol Roger family on the local chalk slopes – identical to those of the best Chardonnay growing areas of Champagne. Now, almost 70 years on, the Hambledon Vineyard spans over 200 acres and produces some of the finest sparkling wines in the world. All of Hambledon's wine is made from estate-grown fruit, and the winery is located on-site, minimising the time between picking and pressing – a crucial factor to ensure the quality of each bottle. They also boast the UK's only fully gravity-fed system, allowing winemakers to produce with minimal intervention. It is decades of these refinements and commitments to lower yield wines that secured Hambledon a Gold award at the 2016 International Wine Challenge for their signature Classic Cuvée. 'Behind the bubbles' tours and private wine experiences are available to book, and are highly recommended.

Hattingley Valley Wines

hattingleyvalley.com
@hattingleywines

In May 2008, owner Simon Robinson had nothing more than some old farm outbuildings and 28 acres of newly planted vines. So, over the following 18 months, he enlisted the help of winemaker Emma Rice to turn his disused farmyard into a modern world-class wine facility. Today, inside those former workshop walls, lies a 500 tonnes capacity winery with over 100 thermo-regulated stainless-steel tanks, 200 Burgundy Oak barrels, a Cocquard press, and an onsite laboratory for fruit analysis.

Hattingley Valley is extremely young by winemaking standards, but ever since those first vines were planted, they have experienced a quite exceptional trajectory. Emma was awarded the prestigious title of Winemaker of the Year in 2014 and 2016 in the English and Welsh Wine of the Year Competition, becoming the first woman to be awarded the title twice. Hattingley was then awarded the 'World Champion' trophy for its 2011 Blanc de Blancs in the Champagne and Sparkling Wine World Championships in 2017.

The Wasabi Company

thewasabicompany.co.uk
@wasabigrowersuk

While visiting one of Hampshire's many watercress farms back in 2010, a chef remarked on how similar the growing conditions were to those of the wasabi fields he had seen in Japan. There, wild wasabi has been grown for thousands of years in well-shaded areas with mild climates, alongside natural springs where the plants thrive off the oxygenated water. Here, Hampshire's many chalk springs and disused Victorian watercress beds provided the perfect conditions – and the Wasabi Company was born.

For those of you thinking about the little green packets from conveyor belt sushi parlours, let me assure you - this is different. In fact, it is thought that less than 5% of global consumption is from fresh Wasabi. The rest is a concoction of mustard powder, horseradish and sweetener and varies wildly from the delicate and sweet plant when freshly grated. You can buy the fresh wasabi online, as well as a range of the company's exciting new products, including wasabi mayonnaise, mustard and vodka.

Page proudly donated by The Winchester Guidebook.

A plan is in place to refurbish an historic building, Burrell House, on the site of the Royal Hampshire County Hospital in Winchester. It will become a dedicated 10 bedded hospice, operating 24 hours a day, seven days a week, to provide much needed local care and support to patients and their families. If you can support our appeal please contact us today.

E-mail: winchester.hospice@hhft.nhs.uk

Online: www.winchesterhospice.com

Telephone: 01962 828353

ALFRED HOMES

A passion for excellence.

In every home that we build, we aim to unite the best house-building innovations with an acute appreciation of legacy. We embrace many period, architectural styles because, quite simply, they stand the test of time - and with an eye for detail, a sense of understated luxury and a commitment to quality - we continually strive to deliver desirable houses you will be proud to call home.

E-mail: info@alfredhomes.co.uk

Online: www.alfredhomes.co.uk

The UK's leading independent real estate consultancy.

Connecting people and property, perfectly is what we do, and it's all thanks to the flawless personal service that we provide to our clients. If you're thinking of selling your property, please contact us for a complimentary market appraisal. Visit our office on Jewry Street, or contact:

E-mail: winchester@knightfrank.com

Online: knightfrank.co.uk/winchester

Telephone: 01962 850333

VOLUME TWO

Initial planning for the next volume has begun. We are delighted to announce that the second edition will be considerably broader in scope with national distribution for the book already secured. We also have some exciting new developments regarding format and photography, as well as additional new chapters on 'accommodation' and 'local interest'. If you would like to appear in the next edition or wish to enquire about advertising, please contact us through the website. We can not guarantee inclusion but will consider all proposals.

www.thewinchesterguidebook.com